THE
Archive Photographs
SERIES

CARLISLE

Two boys locked in a Cumberland & Westmorland wrestling grip watched by an admiring audience. J R Matthews of 251 Warwick Road, Carlisle, took this photograph on the outskirts of the city but the exact location is unknown. The opening of a Cumberland & Westmorland style wrestling academy on Peter Street in 1906 indicates the popularity of this sport. Other photographs in this book show the elaborate costumes worn in wrestling competitions in the city.

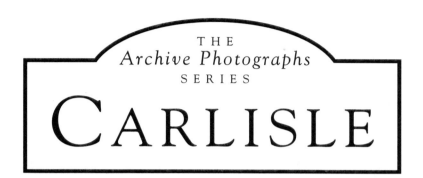

THE
Archive Photographs
SERIES

CARLISLE

Compiled by
Denis Perriam

CHALFORD

First published 1995
Copyright © Cumbria County Council, 1995

The Chalford Publishing Company
St Mary's Mill, Chalford,
Stroud, Gloucestershire, GL6 8NX

ISBN 0 7524 0166 1

Typesetting and origination by
The Chalford Publishing Company
Printed in Great Britain by
Redwood Books, Trowbridge

*Dedicated to Ashley Kendall for his spirited
and untiring efforts to preserve the
photographic history of Carlisle*

Front cover illustration: Jimmy Dyer was a popular figure in the city in the 1890s, often selling his own songs in broadsheet form. Here he is in company with Hugh Bass, the chimney sweep of Kings Arms Lane, at a fair on the Sands. Bottled drinks are on the right hand stall and a potato chip seller attracts custom on the left. The background roundabout advertises 'Exercise With Pleasure'.

Contents

Acknowledgements

I would like to thank Margaret Dick, Matt Browne and Stephen White who read the text and Pat Sanderson who helped in typing it. Carlisle Library, Cumbria Record Office and Tullie House staff were unfailingly helpful in my research for the book. The task of preparing the book would have taken longer without the expert advice of Dr. Patt Honeyman, Ashley Kendall and John Huggon.

I would particularly like to thank Cumbrian Newspapers for permission to reproduce photographs which originally appeared in the *Cumberland News*.

Last and by no means least I must thank the many individuals who have given their photos to the library collection.

Introduction

This selection of photographs is a small part of the 10,000 plus images of Carlisle in the Local Studies Collection at Carlisle Library, a branch of Cumbria Heritage Services. The choice has not been easy as the brief was to use subjects which had not been reproduced before. While most are seen here for the first time, some old favourites have been included to maintain continuity and to give new information on dating and content. Arrangement by street order has been dictated by the way in which the photographs are catalogued and this has proved the most logical way of presenting them. The whole book is a journey through the city and where possible a gradual progression is from one street to another as they appear on the ground. Different periods are presented side by side and this helps to show changes, or lack of them. Reference points have been chosen and then viewed from numerous angles so that a complete picture of an area can be gained.

Seeing the reproductions in this book gives the illusion that the originals are all of the same size and in print form. This is not so. Some of the most exciting subjects are small snapshots taken with a box camera. Many of the lantern slides are contacts from the original negatives and rarely exposed to the light so the quality is superb. The earliest colour photographs in the collection of the 1937 Coronation decorations are large colour transparencies which have not faded. Large format prints were taken by professional photographers with a view to publication for adverts or company records. Others were commissioned by organisations as a record of an important event. Press photographs, often without any information on the print, has meant extensive research through the local papers to find details. Large prints were produced in the Victorian period to be glued into albums while others were small enough to be mounted as carte-de-visites.

Of the numerous postcards in the collection, some have been catalogued by subject and did not appear in the street index and had been largely overlooked. Portrait photographs have also been separately indexed and while most are beyond the scope of this publication, some have been included where appropriate. In all a representative selection has been made to cover as many subjects as possible in order to show the vast range and diversity of the collection.

In the past there had been no library policy of collecting old photographs. The vast majority had been acquired in piecemeal fashion from various donors. If there are too many photographs of buildings in this book, then this reflects what most of the collection shows. Changes towards the collection policy in the 1970s resulted in a photographic street survey which covered the entire city, both old and new. Further work is still required on this before it is really accessible and none of this record has been included in this publication; but it has potential for the future. In the 1980s, publications made the collection better known and resulted in further donations. Purchases, particularly of postcard photographs, have filled some of the gaps in the collection. Other photographs have been loaned for copying. A lively lecture programme in the 1990s has confronted the public with many of the images in the library collection and whetted the appetite of a dedicated audience who would like a more permanent way of viewing the photographs.

One
Market Place

This early 1870s view of a quiet Wednesday market at the Cross differs from a bustling
Saturday. "On a Saturday", as Charles Dickens put it on a visit of 1857, "Carlisle woke up
amazingly and became disagreeably and reproachfully busy". The lamps around the Cross were
meant to light the market, which traded long after dark in the winter, but they were totally
inadequate and had to be supplemented with naphtha lamps on each stall. Prominent in the
background is the Grapes Hotel which was purchased in 1873, along with the lane behind, in
an abortive attempt by the Corporation to create a covered market.

Before: Glovers Row was an island of property which stood in the Market Place separating the Green Market from the general market around the Cross. John Kidd took this photograph in the 1860s from an upper floor window of Thurnams where he had his photographic studio.

After: A much more open Green Market was created by the demolition of Glovers Row in 1897. George Washington Wilson was the Aberdeen photographer who took this view in 1899, and the quality of this and others he took on earlier visits to the city is superb.

Glovers Row had obscured the Crown and Mitre Inn & Coffee House but its demolition brought this into view. The old building, which is where Sir Walter Scott, the novelist, stayed on the night before his marriage in 1797, did not survive for long, being removed in 1903 to make way for the new Crown & Mitre Hotel. At the same time a street widening scheme allowed a better approach into Castle Street.

At the right side of the Crown & Mitre was Spread Eagle Lane, which led to the inn it was named after in the yard behind. The landlord Joseph Johnston, is probably the man on the right. This also came down in 1903 to provide more room for the new hotel. Damage on the negative has caused the strange growth on the roof, which will also be seen on other pub photographs used in this book.

The Green Market, where vegetables were sold, was restricted to an L-shaped site in front of the Guildhall. John & J W Watt, grocers, founded here in 1865, formed part of the end of Glovers Row. Watts moved to Bank Street in 1897 and still trade there today. Women carry open parasols to provide shade in this 1889 photograph by G Whaite.

A Covered Market had been provided by the Corporation in 1854, but this was completely rebuilt on a more extensive site in 1889. Traders were reluctant to move indoors, but further incentive was given by the low extension along West Tower Street for the poultry market, seen here soon after building in 1900.

12

Opening speeches at the Carlisle & Cumberland Horticultural Society flower show, held in the west bay of the Covered Market. The show was at the end of August each year from 1908. Although set aside for country traders on Wednesday and Saturdays, this area of the market was used at other times for meetings and exhibitions. Some of the hats may have been inspired by the occasion!

The pre-decimal prices give a clue to the date of this view of the market in 1968, where bananas were a popular buy. Waltons and Border Fruit Distributors were just two of the fixed stalls which were a feature of the remainder of the market. This part of the market was unchanged until a major refurbishment in the early 1990s.

The interior of the Town Hall was fitted for council meetings, but here, on 9 February 1935, members of a General Workers Committee are meeting to discuss fund raising for the extensions to the Cumberland Infirmary. The hospital was then supported by voluntary contributions and this committee raised £3,675 in a year by holding concert parties and house-to-house collections. T T Hurst took the chair and delegates had come from Penrith and Langholm. The 'Poor box' of 1858, now greets visitors to Tullie House.

William Hurst, Deputy Town Clerk, proclaims the Great Fair on 26 August 1966, in the presence of the Mayor, G J Googan and Sergeant-at-mace. With the decline of street trading the fair lapsed, except for the proclamation ceremony, until the open stalls were revived in 1975. Flower beds which had been intended to beautify the area around the Cross were a great hindrance on such occasions and were later removed.

Two

St Cuthbert's, Blackfriars and English Street

St Cuthbert's Church served one of only two parishes in the city. However, the medieval church was demolished to make way for another and the date of 1778 can be seen on the weather vane of the new building. The formerly crowded graveyard in the foreground closed in 1854 and was cleared of gravestones in 1888. On the extreme right can be seen the backs of buildings on Clarke's Court shown on page 19. Valentine of Dundee took this photograph in the 1890s.

The Farmers Arms was one of a number of licensed premises in St Cuthbert's Lane when this photograph was taken in 1902. Robert Lockerbie, the licensee from 3 June 1901, stands in the doorway and offered dinners for 8d and 1s, as stated on the poster outside. He would do very well on market days. However, he could not make the business pay by 1906 and left, although the licence still had a year to run. Robinson Bros owned the site and their warehouse can be seen beyond. The derelict building was eventually demolished to make way for extensions and their English Street department store. The damaged negative has caused the blemishes at the top and bottom of the print.

The Shakespeare Tavern was another of the pubs in St Cuthbert's Lane, on the same side as the Farmers Arms, but nearer the Market Place. James Allison was the tenant when this photograph was taken and this dates it to between 1913 and 1916. Along with other pubs in the city, this was taken over by the Central Control Board in 1916 and promptly closed down. The rear of Robinson Bros premises on English Street can be seen beyond. This store was extended over the demolished pub site in the 1920s.

The narrow lane leading to St Cuthbert's Church was known as Blackfriars Street, named after the Blackfriars Convent which stood immediately south of the railed churchyard. This 1890s view shows the street before successive widening schemes which meant the removal of the saw maker's on the left in 1927, and the churchyard wall set back in 1935. The properties at the end of the street were demolished in 1903 in connection with the rebuilding of the Crown & Mitre Hotel.

Between West Walls and Blackfriars Street, near the Viaduct, was Carlisle Square. The backs of buildings on Blackfriars Street can be seen on the right. On the shutter on the left of the water barrel, is the trade name of John Lishman, joiner and undertaker, who had premises in the square in 1902 when this photograph was taken.

At the end of Blackfriars Street, near St Cuthbert's Church, was Clarke's Court. The opening into this can be seen in the white building of the photograph opposite and this view looks back towards the same archway. This property and lane were demolished to make way for the Crown & Mitre garage in 1903.

The Market Place decorated for the Diamond Jubilee of Queen Victoria on 22 June 1897. Flags festoon almost every building and the Cross has been specially painted. Between the Cross and James Steel's statue is a temporary platform erected for the Mayor to give a speech as the culmination of the evening entertainment, which included fireworks and a bonfire on the Sands. Behind James Steel is Highmore House.

On 31 March 1931, Redmaynes are advertising a compulsory removal sale because their shop, and that of John Strong, were to come down to make way for Marks & Spencer's new store, opened on 2 October. This had been the family home for the Ferguson's before conversion into shops and Ferguson Lane is between this and the City Picture House on the left. Highmore House on the right, was demolished to extend Marks in 1935.

James Steel has a commanding view of English Street looking south from the Market Place in 1883. Hoardings on the right are for the construction of Jesper's new shop, otherwise there would be nothing to date the photograph because there were no changes in the street until the conversion of Highmore House in 1895. Behind the central cart are railings around the two banks on the Bank Street corners.

Bank Street was newly laid out in 1851, but the south side of the street was not developed until these buildings were constructed in the mid 1870s. The Clydesdale Bank of 1877, designed by George Dale Oliver, is in the centre of this 1890s photograph. On the right is R Harrison's gunmaker's shop of 1878, demolished in 1920 for the Prudential building. Further down are less imposing brick buildings, one of which has large glass attic windows for a photographer's studio.

English Street viewed from the Viaduct corner looking towards the Market Place in 1899. This peaceful scene would soon be disrupted by the laying of the tram tracks down the middle of the street in that year. George Washington Wilson took this and the photograph below.

In this 1883 view from between the Court Houses looking back to the Market Place, almost the full length of English Street is visible. On the left are the gaol corner where hangings formerly took place and the entrance into Blackfriars Street beside the City Arms. On the right is the statue of the Earl of Lonsdale erected in 1845.

The low building next to the Wellington Hotel on the lower photograph opposite, was demolished in 1897 to make way for a new Three Crowns Hotel, seen here between 1911 and 1916. The carved lettering shows that the Old Brewery Company were the owners. On the left is Three Crowns Lane, which in 1904 had been converted into a covered arcade. When taken over by the Central Control Board in 1916, the name was changed to the Citadel Tavern.

The viewpoint of this 1931 photograph is almost the same as that opposite. However changes are evident, the statue was removed in 1929 and the City Arms block demolished in 1930. A single-decker tram is turning the Viaduct corner in this the final year of running.

English Street, Carlisle. 11008

23

The City Arms, later known as the Carlisle Arms, decorated for the Diamond Jubilee of Queen Victoria in 1897. Because this pub was immediately outside the gate to the County Gaol on English Street, it was given the nickname of the 'Gaol Tap'.

The gaol gate opened onto English Street, just to the left of the City Arms photograph above. Over the gate was a clock installed when the new gaol was completed in 1827. When this photograph was taken in 1930, the gaol had closed and the sign on the wall shows that the Federation of Women's Institutes had offices within.

The demolition of the Bush Hotel on English Street to create the Victoria Viaduct in 1877, left an isolated triangular block that ended at the City Arms. J W Johnston, the jewellers, filled the Viaduct corner in this 1928 view. The gaol wall along Blackfriars Street is on the right.

Under State Management ownership, the City Arms became the Carlisle Arms and was stripped of all exterior adornment; only the moulded city arms remained in the pediment. This pub was bought by the Corporation in 1928 so that it could be demolished along with the gaol for street widening and new shops. Woolworths was built on part of the site in 1932, followed by Burtons in 1933.

In 1880 a triumphal arch was placed in English Street between the Court Houses to welcome those arriving in the city for the Royal Show, which was held that year in Carlisle. This was the most impressive of three arches erected to represent the former city gates (that on Scotch Street can be seen on page 55). A further arch was erected at the show gates on Dacre Street. All were photographed by Benjamin Scott, but because of the slow camera exposure, he has had to retouch the blurred flags. A small crowd has gathered to watch the photographer setting up his camera, something few people would have seen on the streets at this time.

Three
Court Square and Citadel Station

Court Square is the large open area outside the Citadel Station, dominated by the imposing towers of the Court Houses, seen here in the early 1920s. The name Citadel comes from the fortification erected here in 1542, to guard the southern approach to the city, which was converted into Court Houses between 1808 and 1814. At the end of the parked cars is the cabmen's shelter erected in 1905. The slope on the left is Court Square Brow which leads to Borough Street and English Damside, past the County Gaol wall. A tram emerges from the trees of the Court Square gardens en route to Botchergate.

When this photograph was taken from Court Square in 1897, the Crescent was still private housing. On the corner with Botchergate, John Boustead had rebuilt the Red Lion Hotel in 1884. Further extensions on the right, had just been completed in 1896. The entrance to the off-sales and bar of the hotel is on the corner, but the rest of the ground floor was occupied by shops. Telephones had been introduced to Carlisle in 1885, so it was not unusual to see a telegraph pole on the top of buildings at this time.

An exhibition of historical material from the area was held in the County Hall, next to the County Hotel in Court Square, for the visit of the Royal Archaeological Society to Carlisle in 1882. Indoor photography was not always successful at this time but Benjamin Scott has captured the essence of the exhibits, which were from various local collections.

Despite heavy rain, a large crowd watched as competitors in the 16th annual MCC London to Edinburgh Reliability Run arrived in Court Square on 19 May 1923. Of the 300 entrants, 126 were solo motor cyclists and one local competitor, No 4, seen in the middle, was Harry Eagene Field Jnr., of Whitehaven, on a 1919 $3\frac{1}{2}$ hp BSA. They had set off at intervals from London at 7pm the previous night and the first arrival in Carlisle was at 1pm (see page 69 for the riders going over Eden Bridge).

Citadel Station has an impressive facade designed by Sir William Tite, which was still to be completed when the building opened to passenger use in 1847. In the foreground, changes in 1931 included new underground lavatories. The railings around the gardens on the right give a date before 1940 when these were removed for the War effort.

The station covered a large area when built and further extensions in 1879 and 1880 made it even larger. A vast overall roof was part of these improvements, but later maintenance problems led to partial removal in 1958. Most of what is shown on this photograph, from about 1905, survives. However the platform numbering was changed and the smoke deflectors replaced by overhead electric wires, and the Station Master no longer wears a top hat.

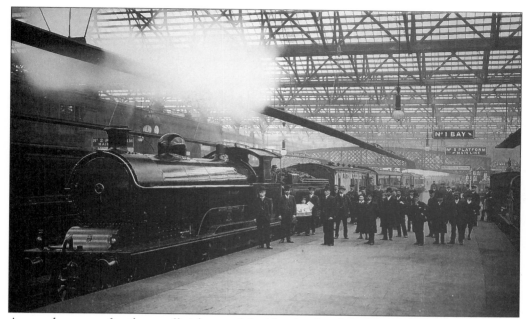

A posed group of railway officials stand beside the London & North Western Railway locomotive 'City of Glasgow', as it awaits departure with a southbound express. A Caledonian Railway locomotive would have pulled the train to Carlisle. F W Tassell has stood in a similar position for this and the photograph opposite. The smoke deflectors are doing their job, but there would still be soot covered glass above.

A group of LMS policemen based at Carlisle, photographed at the station in February 1931. Each railway company had a private police force, indistinguishable from any other except for the helmet badge. Plain clothes detectives and inspectors are at the front. From the medals worn by the other ranks, some had seen service in World War I.

Construction work in progress on the new approach to the station from the north. Workmen on the right, are cutting away the old embankment so the retaining wall for the new alignment can be completed. Decorations on the new Victoria Viaduct, just in front of the County Gaol on the left , show that this was taken on the opening day, 20 September 1877.

Both this and the above photograph were part of the a series taken by Annan & Co of Glasgow, to record the construction of new railway lines into Carlisle in 1877. The newly built Victoria Viaduct crosses the station in this view looking north. Borough Street bridge parapet is on the left, which allowed the old Denton Holme road to go under the station. Further work had to be done on the track layout and a ramp cut through the centre parapet wall of the viaduct in 1879.

For this view of English Damside in the 1890s, the photographer has climbed to the top of one of the retorts in the gas works, seen on the right of the upper photograph opposite. The railway heads north out of the station over the arches (now shops) which are shown on the same photograph opposite. Businesses named on the right include a leather works and Christopher Ling's oatmeal mill. The buildings in the middle were formerly Ferguson's cotton factory and Pattinson's Brewery (whitewashed). In the distance are the Cathedral and St Cuthbert's and St Mary's Churches.

The 'railway nuisance', created by the railway being so close to the Deanery of the Cathedral, seen behind the locomotive, is clearly illustrated in this 1869 photograph. Caledonian Railway No 78, built in 1861 to the designs of the company engineer Connor, stands outside of the engine shed seen on the right, just below the Fawcett Schools. Because of the large driving wheels, these locomotives were known as 'singles'. Railway lines can be seen in the background stretching almost to the West Walls. In advance of building the new approach lines to the station at a higher level in 1877, a new shed was built at Kingmoor in 1874, solving some of the noise problem.

Four
Castle Street
and Abbey Street

It is unusual to find an 1860s photograph of anything other than the Market Place, Castle or Cathedral, so this view of the Green Market corner is of particular interest. The reason for the photograph being taken of what appears to be a fairly ordinary street scene, is because this corner house was the one from which Sir Walter Scott was married in 1797.

The crowded St Mary's graveyard on the north side of the Cathedral had remained disused since closure in 1854 when burials ceased and the new Dalston Road cemetery used. Weathered headstones were removed in 1899, but cutting the grass between those remaining was always a problem. Sheep could graze there in 1925 because of high railings along Castle Street but they were made redundant by a motor mower in 1926.

The fratry of the Priory of St Mary, immediately south of the Cathedral, had ivy clad walls and a flat roof before it was restored in 1880. G E Street, the renowned Victorian architect, designed a new porch and entrance, removing the two external flights of steps just visible amongst the bushes. Internal walls and floors were removed to form a large meeting room and library. A gabled roof was also added to raise the height of the building.

On 4 April 1967, S C Bulley, the bishop elect for the diocese of Carlisle, knocks three times on the door of the Cathedral, to be admitted and enthroned by the dean. The ornate bishop's throne which he was installed in, stands in the choir of the Cathedral.

The carts for the potato market were in Castle Street when this photograph was taken in the 1890s. They had to move from this location when trams came in 1900. The Cathedral railings had been designed by R W Billings in 1838 but were extended on the left in 1866 to include a new gate, later known as St Mary's Gate.

These properties were on the opposite side of Castle Street to the Cathedral in the 1890s. To the left, Atkinson & Davidson's building had been constructed in 1881. In the centre, Watson's decorators, is the only shop that still stands. Behind the two men is the entrance into Carlyle Court. Posters in Coulthard's window show that they were moving to Rickergate and this could give the date of 1892, when the buildings on the right were demolished to make way for new shops that now form part of Bulloughs.

Clement's shop with closing down notices after being compulsory purchased in 1924 for the construction of a new street from Castle Street to Fisher Street. This scheme had been put forward when the Covered Market was rebuilt, but it was not until October 1924 that the new street was cut through. Because this was opposite the gate to St Mary's Church and Cathedral, the new street was named 'St Mary's Gate'.

Thomas Drinkall set up his shop in Castle Street in 1843, after having been a foreman in a large boot and shoe manufactory in Lancashire. The central doorway in Clement's shop above is that seen on the right of this photograph. Drinkall moved into new premises in 1901, seen on the right of the above photograph, and this must have been taken shortly before removal.

Tullie House, the back of which is seen on the left, was acquired for the city in 1890 as an institution to house both library and museum. Extensions, completed in 1893 and seen in this photograph, were for the library reading rooms. George Washington Wilson took this photograph showing the garden layout in the late 1890s, but someone cracked off the corner of the glass negative before the production of this print.

Mrs Hunter stands at the counter in the lending section of the library in about 1923. This was operated on a closed-access system until 1937, so the public were not allowed to see any books before they chose them from the catalogue. The two indicator boards on the counter were meant to save time by showing which books were in or out.

The newspaper room in the library was decorated in 1932 with murals by students at the School of Art, who shared the building. Two tables are set aside 'for ladies only' and a notice on the wall demanded 'silence'. Each morning it was the task of one member of staff to black out the racing columns in the papers, which were considered unsuitable for readers.

On the 22 June 1960, a mobile library service was inaugurated. Here a group of officials pose with the purpose-built vehicle outside the Town Hall before the ceremony.

Castle Street about 1907 on a summer's day with almost all the shop blinds out. The photographer has stood on the corner of Paternoster Row and is looking back towards the city centre. Pedestrians on the right of the street are shaded by the trees in St Mary's graveyard. It is unusually quiet for an afternoon view of a normally busy street. Many of the buildings on the left were demolished in 1965 for Stocklund House.

The bottom end of Castle Street, nearest the Castle, was equally quiet when this photograph was taken from Paternoster Row in the morning, the time given by Tullie House clock. Joseph Walton Hope, a wine and spirit merchant, had the Board Inn on the left, which, with other details, dates the photograph to between 1910 and 1916. The building on the right had been the Girls High School and next to it the Labour Exchange.

Abbey Street in the 1920s had impressive buildings on both sides, but these are not there today. The lower houses were demolished first and the rest went in the 1950s and 60s. The site of the Georgian house behind the railings is today the Salvation Army Barracks. The arch on the right led to stables for Herbert Atkinson House.

In contrast, the top end of Abbey Street, nearest the Abbey Gate, has changed little since this 1890s view. The tall trees in Tullie House gardens on the left have been replaced, but the cobbled street and buildings are the same.

Halfway along Abbey Street, on the west side, was Atkinson's Court. The archway led into Abbey Street. If Sam Bough had not been born there, this building would probably never had been photographed. When a furniture shop was erected on Abbey Street in front of Bough's house in 1896, W Donaldson placed a plaque recording the birthplace with a suitable inscription. The plaque is there today but the court behind has long since gone.

Although Sam Bough spent his early career in Carlisle and received his art training here, he left in the mid 1840s and soon gained wider fame as an artist. He eventually settled in Edinburgh where in later life this photograph was taken. He was president-elect of the Royal Scottish Academy in the year of his death, 1878. Carlisle Library has a collection of his letters and photographs of his painting, which were gathered together by Joseph Pinnington, who was writing a biography of the artist, but never finished it.

Five

The Castle and environs

The Old Black Bull Inn on Annetwell Street stood between the married quarters of the Castle and Irishgate Brow. It was part of a crescent built to improve the approach along Devonshire Walk to the Royal Show, which was held on the Sauceries in 1880. The date must be after 1900 because of the tram lines, but as John Nicholson and William Skelton gave up the licence on 16 June 1902, it may be before then. Because of the illuminated gas sign on the facade, the pub was known by the nickname of the 'Blazing Barrel', but on its takeover by the Central Control Board in 1916, advertising was removed and the name changed to the Irishgate Tavern. It was demolished to make way for road improvements in 1972.

The end of Castle Street decorated for the 1937 Coronation. This and other views of the decorations were some of the earliest colour photographs taken in the city, but reproduced here in black and white. The World War I tank, placed outside the Castle in 1920, was cut up in 1938 in a national movement towards peace when war seemed inevitable. There had been plans to remove the tank in 1926, but an outcry from ex-servicemen had saved it.

On the corner of Finkle Street and Castle Lane stood the Ordnance Arms, so named because it was close to the Castle. Christopher Little was tenant from 1894 to 1897, but the licensee changed so many times after that until closure in 1903, that there was no time to change the name on the outside before this photograph was taken in 1902. The Corporation purchased it for street improvements and the protracted negotiations may have discouraged the Old Brewery Co from spending money on repainting.

The newly laid out gardens in front of the Castle in 1930. This had been intended as a car park but fortunately the Corporation changed their mind. Wooden huts on the left were erected as a recruitment centre in 1916, but these were removed in 1932. There were plans to floodlight the newly exposed Castle in 1933, but it took until the 1980s before permanent lights were installed.

Demolition of the Academy of Art of 1823, seen here in October 1928, opened up the view of the Castle from Finkle Street in 1930. This is a similar viewpoint to the photograph above giving a good before and after impression. The inner ring road now runs over this site.

The entrance gate at the Castle was guarded because it was the headquarters of the Border Regiment. A small garrison was always in barracks here while the rest were serving the Empire. In this 1890s view, the sentry has been joined by a bugler and sergeant major, while ranks of soldiers can be seen on the parade ground through the arch.

Inside the Castle there had been a ditch and half-moon battery to protect the approach to the inner bailey, but in this 1890s view there is no trace of it because it was infilled in the 1820s and gravelled over to provide a larger parade ground. In front of the Captain's Tower is a well which supplied non-drinking water when the ditch was no longer available. The ditch was re-excavated between 1917 and 1919 as part of the restoration of the Castle by the Office of Works.

For garrison use, each building in the Castle was given an identifying letter of the alphabet and in this view from the south ramparts, a K can be seen on the keep. On the right a G can be seen on the Captain's Tower. Changes were made to the letters when a militia store was built in 1881, so the date of the photograph, confirmed by the costume of the girl at the other end of the ramparts, is the 1870s.

'Queen Mary's Tower' after the fire of 18 January 1890. Daylight can be seen through the charred timbers of an upper floor window where the roof should be. The Castle fire engine was inadequate to deal with the blaze and by the time the city engine arrived it was well alight. The building was reroofed and now forms part of the Regimental Museum.

In 1817 a walk was laid out around the Castle walls on land belonging to the Duke of Devonshire, and on the west side it retained the name of Devonshire Walk when this area was built on. When this photograph was taken in 1927, the narrow winding lane led down to the Slaughter Houses, Mayor's Drive and Sauceries.

Robert 'Ginger' Liddle, had his yard behind houses on Devonshire Walk when he was photographed with his son in the 1950s. He moved his business to Nelson Street before the demolition of Devonshire Walk in 1960. His unassuming nature concealed the fact that he had amassed a considerable fortune through his contracting work and interests in horses.

Six
Lowther Street

When this photograph was taken in Lowther Street in about 1897, Jackson Saint's accountants office on the right was a new building. There had been a gap here before 1892 and the ground had been used as a timber yard. The buildings on the left had been built as private houses in the 1820s. This peaceful scene was soon to be shattered by the arrival of the trams.

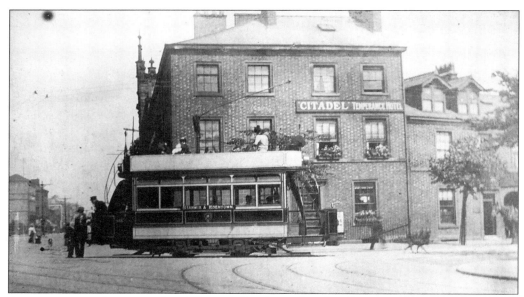

A tramcar turns the corner from Warwick Road into Lowther Street on the route to Stanwix. The pristine condition of the tram indicates that the date is 1900 when the tramway opened. One office worker in Lowther Street complained about the trams in 1911, "the grinding and bumping renders .... conversations or concentration of thought impossible until the car is well beyond the building, then we have a few minutes rest .... when the next car arrives on the scene".

As well as the tram wires down Lowther Street, there were also the telephone wires connected to poles on the right. The National Telegraph Co in Devonshire Street operated the local telephone system and the Post Office the trunk service, until both were amalgamated to be run by the Post Office in 1912. However, the Post Office moved to much larger premises on Warwick Road in 1916 and, as this is an early 1920s view, it seems the telegraph poles were left in place.

A tram passes the Post Office as it travels towards Warwick Road in 1902. Lowther Street was wide enough to have double track for much of its length and it was convenient to have central poles for the overhead wires, but these must have been a traffic hazard in later years. The two men on the left pass Hope & Bendals, wine and spirit merchants, built in 1868 and extended in 1881.

Worthingtons owned the Apple Tree on Lowther Street and it was managed by T & J Minns when this photograph was taken in 1897. Kings Arms Lane is on the left, but this took its name from a pub in English Street. Under State Control, the pub was rebuilt in 1927 to the designs of Harry Redfern and today it is Pippins.

Lowther Street originally ended at Spring Gardens Lane, but a narrow footpath called Eden Street, seen on the right, continued on to Swifts Row and the Sands. Demolition work began in June 1894 to remove the house on the left and properties further down Eden Street, so that Lowther Street could be extended to the newly completed Hardwicke Circus in 1895.

Before Lowther Street was extended, access to Rickergate was along Drovers Lane, seen here in 1923. These buildings were demolished shortly after the photograph was taken, those on the left being eventually replaced by Blair & Palmer's bus garage and on the right by the NAAFI institute. In the distance is the entrance into Warwick Street from Rickergate.

Seven

Scotch Street
and Rickergate

For the Royal Show in 1880, a triumphal arch was built in Scotch Street to represent the Scotch Gate on the city walls, which had formerly stood there. It was one of three gates specially erected for the occasion (see page 26 for the one on English Street). Benjamin Scott, the photographer, has had great difficultly in obtaining a suitable print from the negative because of the waving flags, which were blurred due to the slow exposure of the camera. He has had to heavily retouch a master print and then rephotograph it to make it acceptable to his usually high standards. Some of the buildings on the left, were demolished to build the Market Arcade in 1887.

William Sanderson's grocer's shop was on the corner of Scotch Street and West Tower Street when this photograph was taken in 1928. The buildings are decorated for the Pageant in Carlisle that year. Sanderson was also a photographer and a number of lantern slide views of the city bear his name. The shop is now the Scotch Street Post Office.

Scotch Street in this late 1920s view is relatively quiet and the shop blinds and angle of the sun indicate a summer morning. Ornate gas lamps then graced the entrance to the Market Arcade. At the bottom of the street, can be seen the Singer Sewing Machine sign which is also on the right of the photograph above. The black marks at the top of this print are where the negative and paper were held together in the darkroom.

In 1908 and 1909, the Corporation purchased almost the whole of the north side of East Tower Street for street widening. This involved the demolition of the corner property which had housed Watson's cloggers, seen in the above photograph. After demolition Watson's moved to the newly created corner of Bowmans Court, seen below in 1923. Further improvements to the corner in that year, with a new building which was Grays Art shop, meant Watson's moving again onto the opposite corner, which is Ismay's on the above photograph.

The cyclist appears to have no difficulty in climbing the slope from Rickergate to Scotch Street. At this time Rickergate began at Drovers Lane and Warwick Street. The removal notice in Watson's, the cloggers, gives the date of 1923. Many of the buildings in Rickergate were pubs and the name of the Bay Horse Hotel can be seen behind the girl with a bicycle.

Between the buildings on Rickergate were arches which gave access to the lanes behind. Often these were named after the pubs on the main street and this is Bay Horse Lane, seen in 1937 shortly before demolition.

At the very bottom of Rickergate, opposite the Malt Shovel, was the Drove Inn. Mary Graham took over the licence from William Hall in September 1894 and John Baxter was the licensee from 1897 to 1908, so although this photograph was probably taken in 1902, the name on the signboard was never changed. In August 1916 the Central Control Board took over and closed it in April 1917. The tower of the Civic Centre covers this site today.

Warwick Street was laid out in 1855 by Peter Dixon who had a cotton mill at Warwick Bridge, hence the name of this street and Peter Street at the end. The United bus garage in the distance gives a date of late 1936 or 1937. This street did not remain long after the photograph was taken, being demolished in 1939 to make way for the new combined police and fire station opened in 1941.

A few doors up Rickergate from the Malt Shovel was the Blue Bell Hotel. Today it would be opposite the Civic Centre on a site occupied by the Magistrates Court. Through the arch on the right was Blue Bell Lane which led to the stables. Joseph Black was the licensee from 4 March 1901 and this photograph was probably taken in 1902. A closer study of the posters in the window may date it more accurately. This pub was taken over by the Central Control Board in August 1916 and closed in April 1917 because there were just too many licensed premises in Rickergate.

This panoramic view from Stanwix looks across the River Eden and the Sands towards Rickergate and the city, with St Mary's Church on the left and Dixon's Chimney on the right. As Lowther Street has not been extended through the Sands, the photograph must have been taken before 1895. Just beyond the river on the right, beside the approach to Eden Bridge, is the old auction mart building for the Sands. Under the Cathedral is a large building with the 'Star Music Hall' on the roof, access to which was from Blue Bell Lane shown opposite. To the left of the Star is the Malt Shovel Inn at the bottom of Rickergate.

On the morning of 5 February 1925, the Kingstown bus, operated by J J Foster & Son, crashed into the railings of the Creighton Memorial Gardens near Hardwicke Circus, after skidding on the wet road. Fortunately, the driver, Isaac Foster, was uninjured and no passengers were on board at the time. The company ran three 14-seater buses on the route from their garage in Barley Stack Lane in Rickergate, so the bus would only be a few yards north of the depot. It is probably Mr Foster who is replacing the axle under the watchful eye of a policeman. However, as the registration plate does not correspond with any bus in their fleet it possibly comes from another vehicle cannibalised for the repair.

St George and the dragon surmounted a monument in memorial gardens laid out in memory of J R Creighton in 1898, seen here from Hardwicke Circus shortly after erection. Railings enclosed a triangle of land which had formerly been part of the Sands and was isolated when Lowther Street was extended through to Eden Bridge in 1895. At the end of Corporation Road on the left is the Golden Fleece Inn and Solway Street on the right faces onto the Pig Market. The distant smoking chimney is just beyond the Castle.

With the creation of a new Hardwicke Circus roundabout as part of the Inner Ring Road, the gardens were excavated and the Creighton Memorial rebuilt as a central feature in a new sunken garden. On the 26 May 1971 a workman prepared the base of the column for the re-erection of the recumbent foreground figure of St George, much weathered after its long exposure to the elements.

At 2pm on Coronation Day, 22 June 1911, 47 groups of Sunday school children and their teachers, numbering about 15,000 in all, assembled on the Swifts. Hymns were sung at 3.15, to the accompaniment of three bands, conducted by J P Dowell, who can be seen on the stand using an ebony baton presented to him for the occasion by the Mayor. After each child was presented with a Coronation medal, they paraded their mission banners and flags incorporating a portrait of the new king, George V, through the city centre to their respective meeting places.

Wartime restrictions limited photographs taken in the 1940s, but J Wilkinson managed to sneak this view of William Codona's Super Speedway roundabout on the Sands on 31 May 1941. Servicemen are in uniform and have their tin hats at the ready.

Carlisle was chosen as one of the staging points on the Daily Mail Circuit of Britain and the first aeroplane arrived on the Swifts on 25 July 1911. However, some of the competitors were behind schedule and it was not until the next day that James Valentine in a Deperdussin monoplane landed. He can be seen on his plane with various officials around and cans of oil and petrol ready for refuelling.

Waiting for the planes to arrive was a lengthy business and here a group of spectators have taken armchairs onto a flat roofed building, probably associated with the old racecourse. As many as 25,000 people were estimated to have watched at the Swifts on the first day.

This could show the Easter sports that were held on the land between the river and Castle. On the Castle Bank, from where the view is taken, children would roll their pasche eggs. The background detail and costume suggests a date between 1905 and 1910. This area was known as the Sauceries, thought to be named after the maker of the king's sauces who was granted the land in medieval times.

On 22 June 1911, the Sauceries were crowded for a military parade and open-air service for the Coronation of George V. Taking part were 200 local Territorials, 200 Boys Brigade and 150 Boy Scouts. In the centre can be seen the Rev W P Morris, chaplain to the 4th Border Regiment, who conducted the service. Afterwards each soldier was presented with a shilling to drink the King's health.

Eight
Stanwix and Edenside

Stanwix and Carlisle were always linked by bridges and the present Eden Bridge with alterations, shown in this winter view at the turn of the century, dates from 1815. Amongst the foreground trees is a boundary stone for Carlisle showing that at one time Stanwix was a village beyond the city. Only in 1912 was Stanwix taken into the newly defined boundary. On the left, behind the bridge, is Eden Terrace which can be seen in photographs on the following pages.

This panoramic view of Stanwix from the Castle was taken in the 1890s. On the left is Cavendish Terrace and on the right, behind Eden Bridge, Eden Terrace. In the centre is the tower of St Michael's Church and below that the thatched cottages on Stanwix Bank corner. The Drove Inn, to the left of the church, can be seen when it was freshly lime washed.

Mrs Noble was the licensee of the Drove Inn on Stanwix Bank when this photograph was taken in 1902. Cattle drovers often passed the door on their way from Scotland to the cattle market on the Sands, so the pub was aptly named. Although closed by the Central Control Board in December 1917, the building still stands as a private house today.

Eden Terrace in 1930, which can also be seen on the photograph opposite, was on the slope which originally led to the former Priestbeck Bridge, the forerunner of the present Eden Bridge. The access from Eden Bridge can be seen on the photograph below. This property came down in 1931 so that Eden Bridge could be widened. Gardens were laid out on part of the site in 1933 using stone from the demolished gaol for terrace walls.

A competitor in the 1923 MCC London to Edinburgh run sets off in the rain up Stanwix Bank after a brief rest in Court Square (see page 29). The all-night run had resulted in one rider having to be helped from his machine in Botchergate in a fainting condition; he resumed after an hour's rest. Two policemen in capes anxiously watch for the competitors to avoid any traffic problem the race would cause.

From Stanwix Bank a good view was obtained of the 1890s city. Before the laying of tram lines in 1900, the road surface appears unmade, which must have presented problems in winter and made it dusty in the summer. Gates on the left led to Eden Terrace and on the right to Edenside.

For this view the photographer has set up his camera in an upper floor room of the building which later became Austin Friars School, to look out over Etterby and Stanwix. In the foreground is 'Loshville' and in the distance there are fields where St George's Crescent now is.

Snow on Stanwix Bank in this 1890s view, has made conditions treacherous. It is difficult to see whether one of the carts on the right is being used to grit the road, or has shed part of a coal delivery. Devonshire Terrace in the background was laid out on land belonging to the Duke of Devonshire, hence the name.

This block of thatched cottages stood at the junction of Stanwix Bank and Brampton Road until 1904. The pump in the foreground would have been the only source of water for the families living there as piped water was then only supplied to the city. John Robson would have been aware that this property was to be demolished and took this photograph in 1903.

In this 1923 view looking north towards Scotland Road from Stanwix Bank, the property on the left included the Bird in the Hand pub. This came down for road widening in 1924. On the right, houses on Church Street were demolished in 1931 to improve the approach to the reconstructed Eden Bridge. A tram is turning into Etterby Street at the Crown Hotel.

It is hard to believe that at one time Scotland Road, where the traffic lights are today, was as quiet as this. When this photograph was taken in 1902, there was no fear of being run over by a motor car and the hazards were trams and cyclists. Most people are well dressed, which would be expected in Stanwix, but one boy is without shoes.

The Crown Hotel stood on Scotland Road at the corner of Etterby Street until replaced by a new pub of the same name in 1937. James Wood was the licensee when this photograph was taken which dates it to 1902. The same building can be seen in the photographs opposite. Damage to the negative has caused the dark patch on the right.

The Crown & Thistle, on Church Street, seen here in 1902 and probably taken on the same day as the photograph above, has remained unchanged. This is one of the few State Management pubs which has not been externally altered.

Edenside had been laid out as a cricket ground by 1819 and spectators here have an excellent view of the field from the sloping bank. However, as will be seen on the following pages, they were not necessarily watching cricket. This natural arena was a popular venue for a range of different sports. The costume suggests this is summer and a date around 1910.

A Cumberland & Westmorland Sports Committee met annually at the Edenside pavilion to organise activities for the year, in this instance 1900. Recognisable among the officials are Mr Amos, Mr Maxwell and George Spottiswood (front row, hat off). Mr Spottiswood, who had owned this photograph, had a running ground at the back of the Beehive on Warwick Road in the 1880s and 1890s.

This group of the Edenside Juniors Cricket Team was taken by Benjamin Scott in the 1890s. Many of those shown were sons of businessmen in Carlisle and had successful careers. Eb Gray, later mayor of the city and former owner of the photograph is seated on the left.

The Easter sports at Edenside in 1895 included cycle racing. Some spectators have been allowed onto the field where cricket was normally played, but others watched from the slope below Cavendish Terrace. Screens have been erected on the right to prevent those who had not paid from seeing the event.

Cumberland & Westmorland wrestling drew large crowds when contests were held at Whitsuntide 1899 on Edenside. Judges came from as far away as Newcastle and were distinguished on the field by their bowler hats. This challenge was for the $8\frac{1}{2}$ stone champion. Screens have been erected behind the spectators to prevent unpaid viewing.

Edenside tennis courts were the venue for the North Cumberland Lawn Tennis Tournament. Mixed doubles are being played in 1909 or 1910, but it would seem that the men had the advantage as the ladies were handicapped by their long dresses. One female competitor wrote in 1908 "home again tennis season over for me and that of sewing machine beginning". In the right background is the bath house for Hyssop Holme Well and on the left the building which is now Austin Friars School.

Nine
Rickerby Park and Warwick Road

The north lodge for Rickerby House in 1895. This had been built for George Head Head when he purchased the property in 1835. His coat-of-arms and motto 'Study Quiet' are seen in the pediment. Head's Bank was at the top of Botchergate, so he could afford to live in this large house and maintain the extensive grounds. The gateposts on the left are on the road to Linstock and the house gates are on the right. Later the house became Eden School and the lodge is still there today much the same as in the photograph.

A cenotaph to commemorate those service men and women of Cumberland and Westmorland who had lost their lives in World War I, was unveiled by the Lord Lieutenant of Cumberland on 25 May 1922. The architect of the 40 foot high monument of Shap granite was Sir Robert Lorimer. Carlisle Citizens' League provided the £21,000 to purchase the land for a public park, which had formerly belonged to Rickerby House. The costs include £5,000 for the cenotaph and £4,500 for a bridge. Mayors from the principal towns were accompanied on the platform by the Bishop of Carlisle, the Earl of Lonsdale and sentries who reversed their arms. It was estimated that 25,000 people gathered to witness the ceremony, 60 of whom collapsed during the course of the afternoon because of the hot weather.

To provide access to Rickerby Park from Warwick Road, a War Memorial Bridge over the River Eden was included in the scheme. It was opened at the same time as the cenotaph and this view shows it shortly after completion. The cantilever construction by Redpath & Brown, was so the flow of the river would not be impeded by piers. At the end of the bridge on the right, can be seen the tower of the waterworks engine.

The waterworks pumping engine was housed in a castle-like building at the end of St Aidan's Road. Here it is viewed from the River Petteril. A steam engine inside pumped water from the River Eden along pipes to a reservoir on Harraby Hill. Although disused and stripped of all machinery in 1908, the building stood until 1960.

The waterworks tower was a good vantage point to view the exceptional floods of September 1918. In the foreground, figures stand on the bridge across the River Petteril, which now leads to Stoneyholme Golf Course, but the river has completely disappeared. The distant buildings are on Warwick Road, with the chimney of the Carlisle Steam Laundry and Botcherby beyond. After repeated flooding in the 1920s, the river was deepened and straightened in 1931, in connection with the rebuilding of Botcherby Bridge, but there are still seasonal floods in this area today.

Carlisle Steam Laundry and Carpet Beating Co. viewed from Botcherby Bridge on Warwick Road. This had been built to the designs of T Taylor Scott in 1892, and as the company prospered so its premises were extended; providing useful reference points for dating photographs. The furthest buildings, new stables, were added in 1905, but other additions in 1907 are not seen.

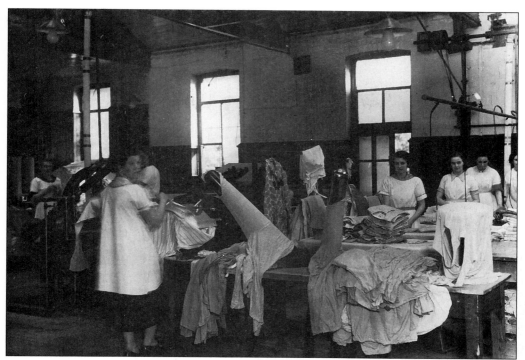

Most of the work inside the Steam Laundry was done by hand and women carried out the more laborious tasks. In this 1940s view piles of collarless shirts are being pressed. The collars were detachable and were cleaned separately so that they could be starched to make them stiff.

The division of labour in the laundry is evident when comparing this photograph with the one above, because all the deliveries were made by men in smart uniforms and caps. It was the men that the customers would see. The specially arranged fleet of vehicles have post-war registrations and as the most recent was registered on 6 May 1949, it seems that the photograph was taken in that year.

Robert Forrester, a designer with the Metal Box Co at their Hudson Scott Branch and a renowned local artist, was asked for ideas for a new badge for Carlisle United. He is here putting the finishing touches to the accepted design in May 1965.

If is difficult to find early photographs that show the Carlisle United ground at Brunton Park, but this is the pitch and stand on 30 July 1910, not long after the club transferred here from Devonshire Park. However, this is not a football match but Cumberland & Westmorland wrestling at the annual Carlisle Sports Day. On the right can be seen the waterworks tower which gives its name to that end of the pitch.

The foundation stone for St Aidan's Church was laid on 20 September 1899 by the Duchess of Devonshire and the building consecrated in 1901. Hoardings behind the church indicates that the photograph may have been taken in that year when the parish hall was under construction.

Our Lady and St Joseph's, the Catholic church on Warwick Road, photographed in the late 1890s, when the trees were newly planted. The church was consecrated in 1893 and as there are no tram lines it is before 1900. Valentine & Co, of Dundee, must have sent a photographer to Carlisle regularly, as this, the above and others reproduced in this book, were all taken on different occasions.

A group of pupils outside the main entrance to Carlisle Grammar School on Strand Road in April 1893. The building was then only ten years old but the school had its origins in the medieval period. Today this forms part of Trinity Upper School following the introduction of comprehensive education in 1969.

George Dale Oliver, 1851-1928, was the Carlisle architect who designed the new Grammar School. His father, Thomas Oliver, was a Newcastle architect and he trained under him before coming a pupil of George Street. He came to Carlisle in 1880 and was later in partnership with E J Dodgshun. For 27 years he was County Architect for Cumberland.

The Duke of Devonshire lays the foundation stone for the new Grammar School on 6 September 1881. Also on the platform was the Mayor, J R Creighton. In the background is the Artillery Volunteers HQ on Strand Road, built in 1874. Behind the brick buildings was a large drill hall which in later years become Carlisle Sports Centre and is now part of Carlisle College.

The Drill Hall in use for the annual Carlisle and District Musical Festival in 1909. The audience have been arranged in the round and there was a useful display of instructions for the competitors. When the volunteers were absorbed into the newly formed Territorial Army in 1908, the hall continued in military use but at times it was let out for other functions.

A High School for Girls had opened on Castle Street in 1884, but it proved inadequate for the number of pupils, so a new building on Lismore Place was built in 1909 at the cost of £18,000. In 1914 when Carlisle became a County Borough, the name was changed to the Carlisle & County High School for Girls. In 1969, it was renamed St Aidan's School, and is today called St Aidans County High School.

As the land on which the High School was built was given by the Duke of Devonshire he was invited to open the building. He is seen on the right, leaving after the ceremony with the architect, Hastwell Grayson of Liverpool, in the bowler hat. The architect presented the Duke with a gilt key enamelled with the Cavendish family crest. This Duke was the grandson of the one who had laid the foundation stone of the Grammar School.

Letters and cards are here being sorted at the Warwick Road Post Office in the Christmas rush of 1924. Many auxiliaries were taken on for sorting and delivery. There was only one post on Christmas morning and no collection until Boxing Day. This GPO had been opened in 1916, but in later years the facilities were inadequate to deal with the Christmas influx and it was necessary to hire temporary accommodation in such places as the Castle and Market Hall.

A peaceful summer's evening scene at the top of Warwick Road in 1951. Billy White, newspaper seller, stands in the doorway of the Newcastle Journal office and 78 inch records are on sale in the window of E T Roberts on the Crescent corner.

Portland Square gardens were formally laid out in 1870 when houses were still being constructed around them. Railings and locked gates ensured that only residents of the square gained access. In the distance on the right is the square chimney of Fendley's Works on Cecil Street; off centre is Rickerby's Chimney on Botchergate.

Sarah Anne Sheldon of 10 Portland Square would have seen the above view from her bedroom. She came to Carlisle in 1847 with her brother, Edward Pattison Sheldon, who was a partner in the crane making firm of Cowans, Sheldon and Co. After her brother's death in 1881, she continued to live in the house he had built in the square and it was here that she died on Easter Day 1920, aged 94 years.

Ten

Botchergate, St Nicholas and Harraby

At the bottom of Botchergate, on the corner of St Nicholas Street and Princess Street, was the Golden Lion Hotel. The exterior was richly adorned with advertising hoardings for the new owners, Messrs Worthingtons & Co, who had acquired the property in 1897. The etched glass bay windows were introduced for the tenants, Thomas & John Minns. This photograph was taken after the completion of the work in 1898 or 1899. Worthington's pubs in the city were taken over by the Central Control Board in 1916 and the adverts removed. Some of the glass remains within the pub today and it retains the same name, but the adjoining housing has since disappeared.

The spire of Christ Church was a prominent feature of Botchergate when viewed from the bottom of the street in the 1890s. Cattle and sheep are being driven to Harrison's Auction Mart further up. On the corner, outside the grocer's shop on the right, had been the first mainland pillar box of 1853, but by this date it was replaced by a wall box nearby.

Joseph Mark, butcher, stands in his apron outside his shop in Portland Place, just off Botchergate. His horse-drawn delivery van and hand barrow, obscure McGeary's hairdresser's shop, next door. Despite the shade offered by the blind, the smell from the open display of meat in the window must have been offensive on a hot summer's day. These shops are there today but have a different appearance to the 1890s.

An early morning scene in 1890s Botchergate. A ladder stands against the front of the Northumberland Arms and an advertising banner hangs from Boustead's Buildings which later became part of the Co-op. On the right is Carrs Bread & Flour Co shop on the corner of Tait Street. Pedestrianisation of this area in the 1990s should create the same traffic free appearance.

Mrs Hannah Deakin owned a pub in Bothergate which had been known as the Jovial Butcher, but she renamed it Deakin's Vaults. When this view was taken in 1902 the licensee was Edmund Bulman who also had the licences for other pubs in the city. This pub was next to the Albion and when the Central Control Board took over in 1916, they closed Deakin's Vaults as the less successful of the two. The building was later demolished to build an insurance office.

Court Street decorated for the signing of the Peace Treaty in July 1919, officially ending World War I. There were parties all over the city, where tables and chairs were brought into the streets and flags and bunting hung from houses. This view is looking towards St Nicholas Street from the Lancaster Street end.

Union Street looking towards Botchergate from the Fusehill Street end in 1937. Back-to-back housing in this street dated from 1824, built by the Union Building Society, so hence the name. When this area was cleared in a late 1930s slum clearance scheme and new council houses built, the name was changed to Rydal Street to get away from the reputation that this deprived street had acquired.

A tram at the London Road terminus decorated for the visit of Princess Louise on 24 September 1908 (see also page 106). On the tram's journey to Newtown, it passed the Cumberland Infirmary where the Princess (daughter of Queen Victoria) was visiting a ward bearing her name, hence the decorations incorporating the word 'Welcome' in coloured electric lights.

When the tramway closed in 1931 most of the track was lifted but it was found to be an unnecessary expense and some was left in place and covered over. Only on St Nicholas Street was a section of track left exposed until a street widening scheme in May 1967 necessitated a new road surface. As can be seen, the process of removal was a laborious task.

Running through the middle of this view is the St Nicholas road bridge. It was partly rebuilt for new approach lines into the Citadel Station from the south, in 1877 when this photograph was taken. The dangerous railway crossing at St Nicholas, infamous for a crash in 1870, is in the foreground and replacement lines at a higher level are seen under construction on the right.

The St Nicholas Bridge was too narrow and as part of an improvement scheme to widen all road bridges in the city, this was rebuilt between 1926 and 1928. This view from St Nicholas Street, looking towards Currock, was taken before work began. Behind the boarding on the left was Cowans, Sheldon & Co and on the right the entrance into builders and slater's yards at Old St Nicholas.

John Hewitson's slater's yard was just below St Nicholas Bridge, on the other side from Cowans, Sheldon & Co. This was on the site of the medieval St Nicholas Leper Hospital. The entrance to the yard can be seen on the lower photograph opposite. St Stephen's Vicarage can be seen behind the trees on the left.

On the same day as the above photograph, 26 August 1932, Alf Johnston photographed this group of employees at Hewitson's, against the wall of St Nicholas Bridge. Third from the left on the front row is the owner F C Atkinson and next to him in the centre, J R Stewart, the manager. Hewitson's also had works at Hexham and at Blackhill near Newcastle.

Cowans, Sheldon & Co, had moved onto the St Nicholas site from Woodbank at Upperby in 1859. This view of their works in about 1907, is from St Nicholas Bridge. The photographer, F W Tassell, touched in the lettering on the buildings so that it stood out and the photograph could be used for advertising purposes.

One of the products made at the St Nicholas Works was this crane for the South African Government. Rail-mounted cranes like this were sent all over the world. The chimneys of houses on Woodrouffe Terrace are on the left and Shadwell Lodge on London Road is partly hidden on the right.

Brown, Tran & Co operated this cotton factory at the Mains on London Road, when this photograph was taken in about 1907. Bendalls now use the remaining buildings as their sheet metal works, renamed the Albion Works. Extensive railway yards in the background belonged to the North Eastern Railway on the left and the Midland Railway on the right.

This view from Harraby Green looks back towards the chimney of the Mains in the left distance and is probably taken at the same time as the above photograph; both by F W Tassell. The Midland Railway waggon repair workshops are in the centre with their Durranhill goods yard beyond.

Between Greystone Road and the River Petteril was Linton Holme hence the name of this pub, built on land belonging to S G & G F Saul in 1899. When this photograph was taken in 1902, Thomas and John Minns were the licensees and the original pub had been extended to include an off-sales on the right.

From the Midland Railway bridge at Durranhill there was a good view of the approaches to the city of the Settle & Carlisle line in about 1907. Extensive railway yards were on either side of the main line, with Durranhill Engine Shed on the left. The North Eastern line from Newcastle is behind the signal box on the right. In the distance is Harraby Hill and Greystone Road area.

Eleven
Currock and Upperby

The South End Co-operative shop, at the corner of Beaconsfield Street and Blackwell Road, was built to the designs of T Taylor Scott in 1890. The South End Co-op had stores throughout the city and branches in other towns in north Cumberland. Along Beaconsfield Street on the right, can be seen the Howie Boyd Mission Hall of 1885, designed by the same architect. Hoardings on the right suggest that work is in progress on the infant block of Bishop Goodwin Memorial School and although someone has dated the photograph 1895, it must have been taken in 1896 when the buildings were extended to Beaconsfield Street.

Ranged along the right side of Blackwell Road, on this view of about 1904, is the Bishop Goodwin Memorial School. The nearest building was the Boys School of 1898 (Girls by 1902) and the original mission school of 1892 is behind the lamp post. Furthest away is the Infant School of 1896. Houses on the left from part of Mulcaster Terrace. An over enthusiastic photographer has left fingerprints on the photographic paper before it was properly fixed.

Currock House had been built with extensive grounds in the 1820s or 1830s. When this photograph was taken in 1937, the land had been sold for housing and part of the new Currock council estate can be seen on Lediard Avenue on the left. The foreground railings are on Lund Crescent. The house was used as a Youth Hostel and Community Centre, with a new recreational hall behind.

An engine shed for the Maryport & Carlisle Railway was built at Currock in 1877, to replace their earlier shed at Bog Junction. This is an Annan & Co photograph of the newly completed building. When the company was amalgamated into the LMS in 1923, the shed closed and was demolished shortly after. Today the only indication that a shed had existed here is the railway housing, Maryport Cottages on Boustead's Grassing, built for engine drivers and locomotive superintendent in 1878.

Michael Young, horse dealer, surveys his estate in about 1910, from his garden at Currock House. Under the belly of his horse can be seen the Glasgow & South Western Railway shed, built in 1895. This was next to the Maryport & Carlisle shed, but survives today as the Currock Waggon Repair Depot.

Children at Upperby Board School in 1896. The owner of the photograph was Mary Agnes Armstrong, shown wearing a shawl on the second row. Her elder sister Jessie is immediately behind her. George Topping, the schoolmaster, wrote with his friend John Potter, as Two Carel Lads, a book of memories of old Carlisle.

Upperby Church was consecrated in 1846 and this 1890s view shows it was very much a country church. Upperby did not become a part of the city until 1912. The extended graveyard around the church has become a cemetery, but the open ground in the foreground is now covered with modern housing.

Twelve
Raffles and Newtown

Land at Raffles was purchased by the Corporation in 1925 to create a new housing estate and part was set aside for recreational use. Dr Heysham, a Carlisle doctor who had died in 1870, left £1,000 to provide a public park and with interest the figure had risen to £2,765 by the 1930s. This money was used to lay out cricket and football pitches, a miniature golf course, a children's paddling pool supplied with water from Parham Beck, ornamental gardens and a community hall, on an area to be called Heysham Park. The hall, seen above, was opened with a gold key by the Mayor, Eb Gray, on 25 August 1934. In his opening speech he asked for "co-operation in preserving this park and hall from any form of abuse or destructiveness". He must have been aware of the vulnerability of the hall, for after repeated acts of vandalism, resulting in serious fire, it was demolished in the early 1990s.

Dalton Avenue in 1937, part of the Raffles Estate. Under the 1924 Housing Act, Carlisle Corporation built 1,518 houses on this estate by 1939, to replace housing in slum areas of the city. The striking thing about this photograph is the absence of cars and the neatly kept gardens, praised in a 1930 guide to the city.

Shady Grove Road took the name of a farm on Newtown Road. This central road ran from Newtown Road to an as yet undeveloped Orton Road. Just out of view on the right would be the newly built St Barnabas' Church. No traffic calming measures were required when this photograph was taken in 1937.

This 1923 photograph, from the corner of what is today Raffles Avenue, was taken to record the view before changes were made. Coledale Hall Farm on the left, was demolished in 1924 and Coledale Hall beyond lost part of the front garden, all for street widening completed in 1925. Other properties on the right were removed soon after when the Raffles Estate was developed. In the distance can be seen the Green Dragon Inn.

William James Mitchell was the owner and landlord of the Green Dragon Inn when this photograph was taken in 1902. He also had a market garden on land behind the pub. Alterations were made in 1905 to replace the stables on the left with a bar extension. Further changes were made under State Control, but it looks much the same today and retains the name it has had since the early 1800s. Light getting in when the negative was exposed has caused the dark corners.

When the Cumberland Infirmary was built in the 1830s, an avenue of trees was planted to improve the view from Newtown Road. When this photograph was taken in the 1890s the trees had matured. However, the Infirmary has now changed, the trees on the left being removed for massive extensions and an extra storey added to the original building. Some of the trees on the right remain.

Princess Louise had visited the Cumberland Infirmary in 1877 when a ward was named after her, but this photograph shows her on a return visit on 24 September 1908. She was accompanied in the carriage by the Earl of Lonsdale and nurses line the steps to greet her. Other nurses view the royal arrival from open windows and left balcony.

Cuthbert Balfour Paul, honorary surgeon at the Infirmary, carves the turkey in the women's ward on Christmas Day 1924. He was assisted by W Theodore Carr, who was chairman of the directors of Carr's Biscuit Company and president of the Infirmary. Balfour Paul died tragically of blood poisoning in Amsterdam in 1926, but is remembered by a ward named after him.

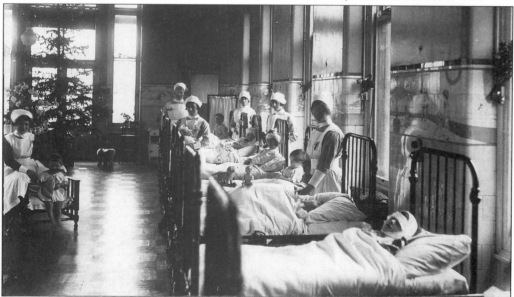

The children's ward at the Infirmary, also on Christmas Day 1924. A similar newspaper photograph shows the other side of the ward where all the beds were also occupied. The boy with his head in bandages on the right has probably had a mastoid operation. On the walls are tiles decorated with coloured pictures of nursery rhymes. Even with the attentions of a devoted nursing staff, these children could not have had a very happy Christmas.

At the junction of Port Road and Caldcotes, the narrow railway bridge carrying the Canal Branch over the road was the scene of a number of accidents involving trams, some with fatalities. Plans for a replacement were first mooted by the Corporation in 1909, but it was not until 14 June 1914 that the old bridge came down. The road was then widened and a new metal girder bridge put in its place. This photograph of the bridge shortly before removal, was taken by Councillor Thomlinson, the prime mover in the renewal scheme.

Thirteen
Caldewgate and Shaddongate

Caldewgate was always prone to flooding and the worst flood was in January 1925 when this photograph was taken in Church Street outside the Joiners Arms. The local press coverage of the event included a pull-out supplement of flood photographs. More views of flooded streets appeared in 1926 and 1927. To alleviate the problems, new drainage pipes were laid along Church Street and Bridge Street in October 1927 and this seems to have helped until the area was again under water in 1968.

An 1899 view from the spire of Holy Trinity Church looking over Caldewgate to the city. In the fork of the road below is the so-called 'Giant's Grave' which was removed to put in tram lines later in 1899. A horse bus from Newtown travels towards town. Carr's Biscuit Factory clock of 1898 is on the left. Smoke from Shaddon Beetling Works drifts across the right of the scene.

The Plough Inn was one of two pubs in Caldcotes when this photograph was taken in 1902. Robert Burns was the licensee, but the building belonged to Lister McCutcheon, a butcher. Behind is the chimney for Carr's Biscuit Factory which can also be seen looking from the other direction in the photograph opposite. This property was demolished to make way for an extension to Carr's in the 1950s.

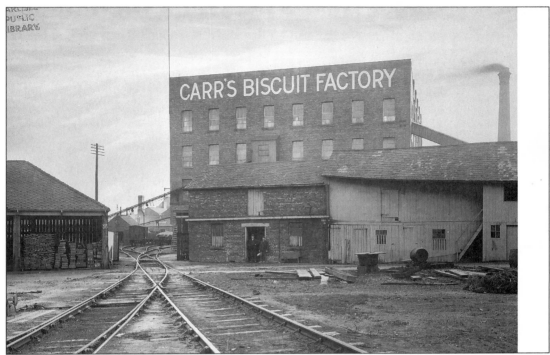

Prominent painted lettering was used to advertise Carr's Biscuit Factory when this photograph was taken in 1907 or 1908. Although at the back of the works and not seen from the main road, the name could be seen from the railway when Carlisle was approached from the north. Traces of the paintwork can be seen today.

In the 1930s many buildings in the city were floodlit, while others were given large, illuminated signs. The first such sign was erected at Carr's in 1931. This 1960s view shows a later neon sign. The building on which it was placed has long since gone to be replaced by a new gatehouse. The same building can be seen on the upper photograph opposite.

111

Opposite the Old Brewery, between Milbourne Street on the left and Brewery Row on the right, stood the Waggon & Horses Inn. As with other photographs taken of pubs in 1902 and reproduced in this book, the name of the licensee is misleading. Noble Harding gave up the licence in 1897 and two licensees later his name still appears on the inn sign. It is probably William Metcalfe, who became the landlord in 1901, standing in the doorway. This pub came down to make way for the widening of Caldew Bridge in 1924.

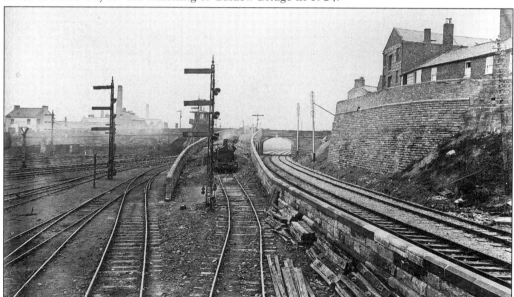

Caldew Bridge, seen in the middle distance of this photograph, was modified to cross new railway lines approaching the Citadel Station from the north in 1877. This shows construction work in progress with the contractor's locomotive on a temporary track which now forms a ramp to the Viaduct Estate. Buildings of the Old Brewery can be seen on the left and the newly constructed passenger lines on the right. The signal box in the centre of the bridge came down shortly after the photograph was taken.

Onlookers watch the early stages of the widening of Caldew Bridge in the autumn of 1924. Hidden from view, but visible from the parapet, workmen were constructing piers in the river below to take the arches for the new roadway. When this was completed in 1925, work began on widening the bridge over the railway, which required the demolition in 1926 of the building behind the horse and cart.

Mr J H Minns, chairman of the Highways and Streets Committee of the Corporation, presents the Mayor, Robert Burns, with a silver replica of the inscription tablet for the reconstruction of Caldew Bridge on 5 November 1925. The ceremony commemorated his involvement in the project and his 35 years service as representative for the Caldewgate ward. The completed bridge was not officially reopened until 28 October 1926.

The Bricklayer's Arms was one of two pubs on John Street, which leads from Church Street to Shaddongate. John Hind Wilson became the licensee on 3 June 1901 and his name can be seen on the sign of this 1902 photograph. Although closed by the Central Control Board in April 1917, the building still stands and had been a private house.

Almost next door to the Bricklayer's Arms was the Malster's Arms Inn. Robert George Pattinson was the licensee when this photograph was taken, probably on the same day as the one above. An illuminated gas star graced the front of the building. This pub was never closed but the facade changed under State Control.

Circling pigeons and some pedestrians are the only sign of life in this view of Kendal Street looking towards Shaddongate. The absence of cars suggests a 1940s date. Dixon's Chimney has its 'top hat' coping, which was removed in 1950, due to its dangerous state. As the land on which this terrace housing was built belonged to Jonathan Dodgson Carr, founder of the biscuit works and born in Kendal, he named the street after his birthplace.

This Tassell photograph from West Walls looks across the Viaduct Goods Yard to Milbourne Street, Shaddongate and Caldewgate. It was probably taken in 1907 or 1908. Prominent on the left is the Shaddon Works and Dixon's Chimney. The New Brewery kilns and roof tops are on the right, with the Trinity Church spire in the distance.

In this 1937 view, the junction of Richard Street and Milbourne Street can be seen. It is almost a continuation of the photograph opposite and was taken on the same day. Much of the former back-to-back housing shown, has been modernised and is still lived in today. In the distance is the former Charlotte Street Congregational Church.

The Denton Holme millrace flowed through Shaddongate and it can be seen behind the railings of this 1937 photograph. Although called Shaddongate today, the foreground cobbles were part of Caldew Terrace. Beyond the millrace is Brewery Row, which led from the Old Brewery to the New Brewery. On the right is Richard Street which can also be seen below.

Richard Street gave access from Milbourne Street to Brewery Row. This 1937 photograph shows the slum property shortly before demolition. At the end of the street can be seen the New Brewery offices and behind those Shaddon Beetling Works on Shaddongate. Not a single building on this view can be seen today.

The Old Brewery Co owned the Lorne Arms in Shaddongate when this photograph was taken in 1902. Broadguards is the street on the right. John Skelton was the licensee from 4 March 1901 and he is probably the man in the doorway. The taller man on the right is so dirty that he could have been a chimney sweep. In the window are posters which advertise Samuel Franklin Cody appearing in "Klondyke Nugget", which are misleading as this was performed in the city in 1899 and it seems that these were used long after the event to attract customers to the otherwise uninteresting display of bottles. Although taken over by the Central Control Board in 1916 with a view to closure, the pub continued to trade until the early 1920s and was sold as a house and shop in 1924.

Fourteen
Denton Holme
and Wapping

Thomas Minns stands with hands on hips in his shop doorway on the corner of Thomas Street in the 1890s. Major Thompson of Milton Hall purchased this site, close to the railway bridge over Denton Street, in 1870 when it was Brockbank's saw mill, to construct a coal depot for the Naworth Collieries. He engaged the architect, George Dale Oliver (see page 84), to design a terrace of houses and this shop on the remaining land. These were completed by 1885. In 1994, the long disused shop was converted into a house.

Keen's grocers shop stood on Norfolk Street at the entrance to Carrick's Hat Factory when this photograph was taken in the 1930s. It is another of the corner shops in Denton Holme now converted into a house.

Beyond Robert Ferguson School on Denton Street, land for building houses was purchased by the Corporation in 1915-16. By September 1921 twenty four council houses were occupied. This photograph shows the well established trees in 1937.

The Prince of Wales on Denton Street, dated from the laying out of the street in 1852-3. There was also a bowling green and this may have been where the Star Cinema was later built. This was taken in 1902.

A view from Blackwell looking towards Denton Holme in the mid 1890s. In the foreground is the Maryport & Carlisle Railway between Cummersdale and Currock. The tall chimney on the left is part of Ferguson Bros Factory and beyond that the large houses on Norfolk Road and St James Church.

Ferguson Bros Factory at Holme Head was on the site of an earlier textile works which had been established there to make full use of the water from the River Caldew. The dam across the river on the left, was the source of the Denton Holme millrace, which ran through the factory and originally powered the machinery, but when this photograph was taken in about 1907, all power was by steam, thus necessitating the chimney.

A combined coffee house and recreation room was built on the corner of Bridge Terrace and North Street to the designs of T Taylor Scott in 1881. Ferguson Bros provided this and a bowling green for their employees. The distinctive octagonal building still stands today, but the factory chimney (also seen on the views opposite) on this pre-1900 view has now gone.

Mr & Mrs F W Chance are returning home to Morton Manor on the 22 April 1909. Mr Chance, later Sir Frederick, was director of Ferguson Bros and had inherited this house from his uncle, R S Ferguson, in 1898. As the company had business interests in the USA, it is possible that they are returning from a visit abroad.

Nelson Bridge was built in 1852 as a more direct route between the city and Denton Holme. When new railway goods lines were laid through this area in 1877, the old bridge was raised to be incorporated into a new high level road. On 20 September 1877, this new viaduct, named after Queen Victoria, was opened by her daughter Princess Louise. The triumphal arch seen on the viaduct was decorated for the opening ceremony.

An Electric Lighting Station was built on James Street in 1899 and this is the new engine room of the works. Coal-fired boilers produced steam to power the generators. This became redundant when the new Power Station opened at Willow Holme in 1927. These buildings continued in use as offices, stores and a maintenance depot for NORWEB until they moved to the Hadrian Mill in 1986, which had been built on the site of the bowling green opposite.

Opposite: Murrell Hill House and grounds, the former home of Thomas Nelson (the person the bridge was named after), were purchased as a site for the expansion of the Morton Sundour Factory in 1900. Instead of demolishing the house, it was used as a recreation centre for the workers at Morton's Denton Hill Works and the grounds laid out for sports. This is the opening of the bowling green on Blencowe Street in 1928 by Sir James Morton and his wife, watched by R D Denman and J H Brackenridge.

Much of the remaining housing in Wapping was cleared in the 1960s. Here in July 1966, property on Currock Street, between Crown Street on the right and South John Street behind the lorry, is being demolished for street widening.

The Goliah Inn, on the corner of Robert Street and Crown Street, photographed in 1902, was named after a locomotive used on the Newcastle and Carlisle Railway. When the pub was modernised by the Central Control Board in 1917, the name was changed to the Goliath. It remained open until 1938.

St Stephen's Church stood between Hewson Street on the right and St Stephen's Street on the left, fronting onto James Street. The church was consecrated in 1865 and served the Wapping area. F W Tassell, who took this photograph about 1910, was not happy with the sky and has superimposed the clouds from another negative. The church was demolished in 1965 and the bells taken to use in the new St Elizabeth's Church at Harraby.

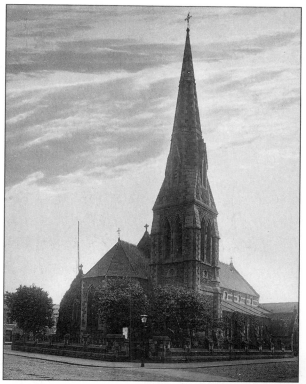

In this 1937 photograph, the doorway on the right was opposite the Goliah Inn on the corner of Robert Street. This view, looking from Crown Street towards the Hudson Scott Branch of the Metal Box Co, shows old property about to be demolished in a slum clearance scheme at that time.

Henry Bannister took many portrait photographs in his Warwick Road studio in the 1850s and 1860s. He made up composite groups like this one and numbered each person with a key giving their names. Most of the individuals were well to do, such as the Dean and Bishop in the centre and the Duke of Roxburgh and Lord Brougham. The photographer regarded himself as an 'artist photographer' and was suitably dressed for his portrait, third from the left at the bottom. Amongst his fellow artists included are Matthew Nutter (46) and David Dunbar, the sculptor (66).